THE SARCASTIC SPORTS TRIVIA BOOK

THE SARCASTIC SPORTS TRIVIA BOOK . . . . .VOLUME 1

THE SARCASTIC SPORTS TRIVIA BOOK

300 FUNNY AND CHALLENGING QUESTIONS FROM THE DARK SIDE OF SPORTS

AN IRATE FAN—PAUL NARDIZZI
with special help from the proliferation of idiots in the sports world.

Writers Club Press
San Jose New York Lincoln Shanghai

THE SARCASTIC SPORTS TRIVIA BOOK
300 FUNNY AND CHALLENGING QUESTIONS
FROM THE DARK SIDE OF SPORTS

Writers Club Press
an imprint of iUniverse.com, Inc.

For information address:
iUniverse.com, Inc.
5220 S 16th, Ste. 200
Lincoln, NE 68512
www.iuniverse.com

ISBN: 0-595-19619-5

Printed in the United States of America

To Bryant, Bryce, Jared and Elena.

ACKNOWLEDGEMENTS

I would like to thank myself for doing all the research on this book. I would also like to thank the athlete's for being such boneheads. If it weren't for your greed and incredible folly this book would not have been possible. I truly hope that I have offended each and every one of you.

CONTENTS

Acknowledgements vii

THE SARCASTIC SPORTS TRIVIA BOOK xi

BOXING 1

NBA BASKETBALL 13

DIVISION 1 COLLEGE BASKETBALL 25

HOCKEY 37

BASEBALL 49

FOOTBALL 63

DIVISION 1 COLLEGE FOOTBALL 75

OLYMPICS 89

WUSSY SPORTS (SOCCER, GOLF, TENNIS) 103

MISCELLANEOUS 115

About the Author 129

THE SARCASTIC SPORTS TRIVIA BOOK

This book contains 300 questions to challenge your knowledge of sports, drugs and thugs. The trivia covers a variety of topics: actual sports (football, hockey, baseball), tycoon distance walking (golf), drug induced competitions (Olympics), lame hobbies (tennis, soccer), public executions (boxing), suicides (auto racing) and cold blooded murder (horse racing). Use the chart below to gauge your lack of knowledge. On questions where there are multiple answers, give yourself credit if you get fifty percent or more correct. Then go crying home to your Mommy. Please note that there are tiny cameras planted within the pages of the book. Any person caught cheating will be summarily beaten about the head with a special hardcover version of the book by a drug induced NFL lineman.

Author's note: The highest scores are not typically obtained by trivia geeks, but rather by folks who rub elbows with athletes on a daily basis, such as Superior Court judges, parole officers, wardens, strippers, pharmacists, hookers and jacuzzi installers.

SCORE	ELEMENT
250-300 CORRECT	GOLD MEDAL
200-249	SILVER MEDAL
150-199	BRONZE MEDAL
100-149	URANIUM BUNDT CAKE
50-99	MUG OF SULFURIC ACID
0-49	RETURN BOOK FOR REFUND

BOXING

---

1) Despite not being able to remember the feat, five boxers have defeated Muhammad Ali and done irreparable damage to their cerebellum. Who are these pus infected peabrains?

2) Who is the only fighter to win Ring Magazine's Fighter of the Year in the 1980's and twice in the 90's? Hints: He dalk like dis. He also holds the unofficial record for most children fathered in a three week span with a total of 19. He doesn't know their names, but with the help of a psychic, is able to point to their general whereabouts on a large globe.

3) Only one fighter in history has held belts in five different weight divisions in his career. Who is he? Hints: He also held 23 retirement press conferences over a ten month span. He was also so adept at impressing the judges with his fancy footwork that they rarely noticed the massive beating his head was absorbing. He retired for good in 1998 and is due to return in 2005.

4) What butt ugly heavyweight is credited with the most knockouts ever? Hint: Several came seconds before the final bell and a couple came several minutes after it.

5) Can you name the only cauliflower-eared heavyweight champion to also hold belts in two lower divisions at some point in his career?

ANSWERS

BOXING

1) Ken Norton, Joe Frazier, Leon Spinks, Trevor Berbick, and Larry Holmes.

2) Evander Holyfield or "Ebander Howypeeled"

3) Sugar Ray Leonard

4) Archie Moore with 130

5) Bob Fitzsimmons (1897-99) who also held light-heavy (1903-1905) and middleweight belts (1881-1897).

SCORE_____

BOXING

6) Name the five men who have won the light heavyweight title and were also chicken-shit enough to move down to win belts in two lower weight classes. Hint: Each had a heart the size of a Tic Tac.

7) Ring Magazine has named the Fight of the Year every year since 1945. The shortest of these fights lasted less than two rounds and cost me five G's plus my house. Which two fighters were involved in the bout that placed me on welfare?

8) Who was the first fighter to lose the heavyweight title and then win it back? Hint: He won it back against the same man who took it from him, because revenge is a mortal sin and he knew he was going straight to hell anyways, along with everyone else involved in boxing.

9) Who was the last fighter to lose the heavyweight title and then later read the latest WBA script and find out he was going to win it back? (I stretched the truth a bit on this one. Actually his manager read it to him while this chowder brain sat on his manager's lap and complained that there weren't any pictures.)

10) Only one heavyweight in history has lost the title and then regained it in the same year. Who benefited from this fix?

ANSWERS

BOXING

6) Sugar Ray Leonard, Thomas Hearns, Iran Barkley, Roy Jones Jr. and Mike McCallum

7) George Foreman's 2nd round knockout of Joe Frazier in 1973 netted me a weekly check of $34.67

8) Floyd Patterson did what the mafia told him to do (lost to Ingemar Johansson) in 1959 and wisely listened again (regained the belt in 1960).

9) Lennox Lewis acted out a loss to Oliver McCall then beat his head sideways in a rematch that was written and directed by Don King.

10) Muhammad Ali did it by beating Leon Spinks in 1978, despite constantly getting his gloves lodged in the space between Leon's incisors.

SCORE_____

BOXING

11) Since Mike Tyson won the heavyweight title in 1986, six stiffs, not including Robin Givens, have been KO'd in the first round against the gold toothed rapist from the Catskills. Who are these six brain-damaged Alzheimer patients?

12) Two of the ten biggest upsets in fat shit (heavyweight) history (based on betting odds) have taken place in the home of another heavy-weight—Babe Ruth. Which two upsets took place in Yankee Stadium? Hint: The fights were won by white fighters, hence the "upset".

13) Of all the champions, who is the fattest piece of shit ever? Hint: Instead of a corner stool, this lummox used to sit on a LA-Z BOY recliner while his corner men fanned him and fed him freshly picked grapes.

14) There have been two other repugnantly fat titleholders in the heavy-weight division who each weighed over 250 pounds. Name these saggy pectoraled disgraces to humanity.

15) Can you name the last man to weigh under 200 pounds when he took the heavyweight title? Hint: He would have weighed 210 but he was missing several teeth and a vital organ known as the brain.

16) Who is the last man to win the heavyweight title by successfully concealing a metal object in his glove (Knockout)? Hint: He is the only known preacher whose side job is to go around pummeling innocent individuals for a few shekels.

ANSWERS

BOXING

11) Henry Tillman, Peter "who turned the lights out" McNeeley, Bruce Seldon, Alex Stewart, Carl Williams and Mike Spinks.

12) Joe Louis was embarrassed by Max Schmeling in 1936 and Floyd Patterson was utterly humiliated by pasty white Ingemar Johansson in 1959.

13) Primo Carnera jiggled in at 270 pounds of quivering cellulite in his 1934 title defense.

14) Lennox Lewis and George Foreman. Lennox may not look fat due to the fact that you can't see between his ears. Foreman looks fat because he has a substance known as fat covering his entire body.

15) Leon Spinks when he snorted himself down to 198 to beat Ali in 1978.

16) George Foreman when he knocked out Michael Moorer in the 10th round of their 1994 bout. Foreman capitalized on the event by exposing the metal object which led to his being a spokesman for "Meineke Muffler".

SCORE_____

6

BOXING

---

17) Excluding mega-stiff Frans Botha, who was stripped of the title for steroid abuse, name the last oxymoron (white fighter) to be heavyweight champion. Hint: His signature move was to throw harmless jabs while thunderous hooks, crosses and uppercuts rained down on his empty head. Then, at a precise moment in the fight, he would unleash a hook of his own and wake up in a hospital bed with a broken face and IV's going into his cerebral cortex.

18) If you know the answer to number 17 then you might recall the man who brought reality back to Don King's storyline (he KO'd the white bum) in round eight to take the title. Hint: You're looking at one. He recently fought in 2001 at the ripe age of 46 and held his own—especially considering he was in a wheelchair.

19) Not counting his dignity, Roy Jones has only one loss in his career. Who defeated him? Hint: The term "defeated" is used lightly as Roy actually pounded the shit out of the sorry bastard, but was disqualified just in time to save the hemorrhaging bastard's life and create another money making scheme known as a "rematch."

20) Who slapped the bejeesus out of every tomato can along the way to holding the heavyweight title for a record 11 consecutive years? Hint: His typical fight plan was to come out in round 1 and measure his feeble opponent by throwing a half hearted jab into the coward's face. The champ would then retreat to his corner, don his robe and ride home in a limo with yet another knockout victory.

ANSWERS

BOXING

17) Gerrie Coetzee in 1983.

18) Greg Page in 1984.

19) Montel Griffin in 1997.

20) Joe Louis from 1937-1948.

SCORE_____

BOXING

---

21) Name the empty headed mulyak who now drinks pork through a straw as a result of getting his head beat in a record total of six times in heavyweight title bouts? Hint: Similar to other boxers, after his career ended he went on to do absolutely nothing.

22) True or false. A teenager has held the heavyweight title. Hint: You have to pick true or false.

23) Who is the oldest coot (37) to win his first heavyweight title. Hint: His fighting strategy was to bleed all over his opponent for fifteen rounds and then hope the judges became confused about the origins of the sanguinary mess displayed in front of them.

24) Which gap-toothed imbecile held the heavyweight belt the most consecutive years in the second half of the 20th century? Hint: He did it by refusing to fight anyone until they were either 47 years old, were in the early stages of Alzheimer's or were missing a limb or two.

25) In 1976 a total of five U.S. fighters won gold medals. Only one of them did not go on to win a pro title, choosing instead to sit on a porch for days on end drinking beer and passing wind. Who was this waste of talent? Hint: He was named the Outstanding Fighter of the Games.

ANSWERS

BOXING

21) Jersey Joe Walcott

22) False. Mike Tyson was 20 when he became the youngest, most immature champ ever.

23) Jersey Joe Walcott was 37 when he caved in Ezzard Charles's head in 1951. Charles was 93 and entered the ring confined to a bed with his legs elevated.

24) Larry Holmes from 1978-1985.

25) Howard Davis

SCORE_____

BOXING

26) Name the heavyweight who has the highest knockout percentage of all time. Hint: He did the punching, not the computing.

27) Six men have won Olympic gold for the U.S., then later got hypnotized by Don King (turned pro) and won the heavyweight title. Name them. You really have nothing better to do if you can name the two who fought as corpulent bastards with eating disorders (Olympic Super Heavies).

28) In 207 official career fights and countless others with his wife, Sugar Ray Robinson was knocked out only twice—including once in the kitchen with a frying pan. Who knocked him out in the ring and what was significant about the fight?

29) There have been only two lightweights who have held the title for six straight years. Can you name these punchdrunk morons? Hint: One would smile at his opponent after a vicious body shot. The other would curl into a ball crying out in pain while his corner rushed in with buckets of Mylanta.

30) Name the incompetent shit-stain who held the unanimous heavyweight title the shortest amount of time (11 1/2 months). Hint: His typical fight plan was to get his opponent in the corner and then smother him in a pile of fat and tits until the man's lungs exploded or he had an orgasm.

ANSWERS

BOXING

26) George Foreman

27) Muhammad Ali, Floyd Patterson, Mike Spinks, Leon Spinks, George Foreman and Joe Frazier. (Foreman and Frazier fought in the heavyweight division.)

28) Joey Maxim. It was Sugar Ray's last fight in a boxing ring. He had thousands more in the pantry, parlor, bedroom, garage, car, and church pew.

29) Roberto Duran from 1972-1979 and Benny Leonard from 1917-1925. Leonard retired as the champ while Duran continues to fight dementia patients at various nursing homes around the country.

30) Primo Carnera held the belt for only 11 1/2 months from June 29th, 1933 to June14th, 1934. Upon losing he exclaimed, "What's for dinner?"

SCORE_____

NBA BASKETBALL

1) Who is the only player in history with both 2,000 career steals and 2,000 blocked shots followed by the proverbial shout of "yo mama eats shit"? Hint: His signature move is to get his opponent in the air with a nice up fake, then instead of laying it in for two, the overgrown musclehead continues up faking until the shot clock buzzer goes off.

2) Who is the last player to win MVP of the NBA Finals playing strictly a forward position? Hints: He's also played the forward and rear positions with several hookers. He wore goggles, not because he didn't see well, but rather because he didn't want the authorities to recognize him.

3) Because NBA players lack the heart to come back from 2-0 deficits, there have been six 4-0 sweeps in NBA Finals history. Name the winning coaches in these horrendously boring series.

4) Name the only franchise to quit (be swept) three times in the finals.

5) Name the three Boston Celtics' coaches who have won titles by sitting on the bench watching Hall of Famers play and also had their asses wiped in the finals while coaching a shitty NBA team.

ANSWERS

BASKETBALL

1) Akeem Olajuwon. His blocks are unique in that he always swats the ball in the direction of Mecca. During Ramadan he abstains from running up and down the floor and playing defense.

2) James Worthy in 1988. If you guessed Tim Duncan—he played center and forward.

3) Red "Stogie Breath" Auerbach, Chuck Daly, Al Attles, Billy Cunningham, Rudy Tomjanovich, and Larry Costello.

4) The Minneapolis and Los Angeles Lakers franchise mailed it in during the 1959, 1983 and 1989 finals.

5) K.C. Jones (Wash. Bullets-1975), Red Auerbach (Wash. Capitols-1946) and Bill Fitch (Houston-1986).

SCORE_____

NBA BASKETBALL

6) Who are the four ugly white bastards who were voted Finals MVP by a staff of writers wearing white hoods and burning crosses up in the press box? Hint: A group picture of these players looks very similar to drawings depicting the evolution of early man. A group picture of the writers looks very similar to a Klan meeting.

7) Who is the only bug-eyed freak to terrify fans in the front row and win the Finals MVP with two different clubs? Hint: When he padded naked into the locker room shower his teammates would come running out with cell phones screaming "get me the number for the National Enquirer."

8) Two teammates once copped co-MVP honors in the annual marketing abortion known as the NBA All-Star Game, because the other players chose to rest so they could win games that actually matter. Who were these useless teammates?

9) Which two players won NBA scoring titles when Michael Jordan was playing minor league baseball, golfing with mafia guys, opening restaurants and screwing on the deals when they went south, doing commercials, gambling, flying around the world, traveling through space, making shitty films, producing cologne and underwear, smoking cigars in strip clubs, hawking frankfurters, buying NBA franchises, beating the snot out of Steve Kerr, making public speeches defending the loss of lives as a result of his $129 dollar sneakers that cost three cents to manufacture, practicing his traveling and palming moves, and spending tons of quality time with his family?

ANSWERS

BASKETBALL

6) Jerry West in 1969, John Havlicek in 1974, Bill Walton in 1977 and Larry Bird in 1986 all accepted the award presented by the Grand Wizard.

7) Kareem Abdul Jabbar (1971 & '87—the first MVP award was won in his pre-towel head days when he was named Lew Alcindor).

8) John Stockton and Karl Malone in 1993. (Also known as S & M, because they tease and abuse their fans but never fulfill their needs.)

9) Shaquille O'Neal in 1995 and David Robinson in 1994.

SCORE_____

NBA BASKETBALL

10) Who is the last white player to win the NBA scoring title, despite loud protesting from the NAACP? Hint: His signature move was to draw a quadruple team and then force up a fading, one handed prayer between his legs because his teammates were useless sacks of shit.

11) Who are the only two men to pick up whores and win rebounding titles in three different cities?

12) Name the only city that has seen four different players win a rebounding title. Hint: The subway picks you up downtown and drops you off in the middle of a knife fight.

13) Since 1980 only two white players have defied the laws of genetics to win NBA rebounding titles. Who are these two pasty-faced clods?

14) Because Utah's stat man thinks John Stockton's air balls and bricks are actually alley oop passes, John was able to win nine straight assist titles. Who stopped his run by playing in a city with another dumb assed stat guy?

ANSWERS

BASKETBALL

10) Pete Maravich of the New Orleans Jazz in 1977 with a 31.1 average.

11) Dennis Rodman in Chicago, Detroit and San Antonio. Wilt Chamberlain in L.A., Philadelphia, and San Francisco.

12) Philadelphia with Charles Barkley, Wilt Chamberlain, Neil Johnston, and Moses Malone.

13) Bill Laimbeer in 1986 for Detroit and Swen Nater in 1980 for San Diego.

14) Mark Jackson in 1997 with an 11.4 assists per game average.

SCORE_____

NBA BASKETBALL

---

15) Who is the tallest player ever to win the assist title? Hint: He claimed to have slept with over 10,000 women (and I thought 8,000 was a lot). A recount was taken, but was inconclusive as most of the women had private areas that were dimpled or were covered with hanging chads.

16) Who is the only player to win assist titles for three different teams? Hint: He was constantly being traded from one foul smelling venue to another and eventually wound up in the stench capital of America.

17) Who is the last white player to lead the league in steals? Hints: He honed his skills in the off-season by stealing car radios and my wallet. He played in the 70's and used to shower with his cup on.

18) Can you name the team of chokers that has made eight appearances in the Finals and only won two of them? Hint: Despite losing six series, the players still gyrated their hips and whooped it up every time they closed the deficit to 36.

19) Who had the highest field goal percentage ever for a single season? Hint: He wore a velvet jock strap and housed his testicles inside a four liter cup.

ANSWERS

BASKETBALL

15) Wilt Chamberlain in 1968 with 702 assists.

16) Kevin Porter for Detroit, New Jersey and Washington '78, '79 and '81. (Gee what great stops.)

17) Don Buse for Indiana in 1977. Also known as Don A-Buse-d for his defense.

18) New York Knick(erbockers)

19) Wilt Chamberlain in 1973 for L.A. with a .727 percentage.

SCORE_____

NBA BASKETBALL

20) Only once in the 80's did the FG percentage leader fall under 60% because dunking is easy, especially if you can jump through the ceiling cuz you're all hopped up on crack. Name the drug abused vermin who failed to reach the 60 percent mark.

21) Who is the only player to lead the league in the exciting free throw percentage category more than three years in a row? Hint: When he looks back at the memories of his life all he sees is a white line, a leather ball and some clown in a striped shirt. Everything else is a complete blank. He currently travels the country lecturing young players not to waste their fucking time.

22) The only player in history to average over five blocks a game was so busy blocking shots he never bothered to learn how to shoot, rebound, pass and breathe. Who is this sucky big man? Hint: His large white ass parked in the key may well have been the inspiration for the three second violation.

23) Name the two University of North Carolina guards who won back to back NBA Rookie of the Year Awards in 1978 and 1979. One had a decent career and the other should have quit while he was ahead.

24) Who is the only guard to win Rookie of the Year after being chosen number one in the draft? Hint: (Career stats: 2,387 shots, 45 tattoos, 3 passes, 1 DUI, 1 Governor's pardon).

ANSWERS

BASKETBALL

20) Dennis Rodman in 1989.

21) Bill Sharman from 1953-1957.

22) Mark Eaton "Some Leather" of the Utah Jazz with 5.56/game in 1985.

23) Walter Davis and Phil Ford

24) Allen Iverson was drafted by the '76ers in 1997. He wasn't able to attend the ceremony because he was swerving around in his car smoking dope and firing off shotguns.

SCORE_____

NBA BASKETBALL

25) Who is the only coach to be named NBA Coach of The Year despite having a worse record than the previous year? Hint: He also has the same track record as a General Manager, getting shittier and shittier as the years pathetically drag on.

26) Can you name the only coach on the 50th Anniversary of the NBA's list of 10 Greatest Coaches whose career was a complete waste of time (never won a title)?

27) Can you name the only coach on the list of 10 Greatest Coaches in NBA history to not belong on the list (have a winning percentage under .500)? His coaching philosophy was to run the good players out of town so his team could suck, and then draft high and get more good players to run out of town. He kept this cycle going for ten solid years.

28) Which overpaid maggot holds the record for the highest steals per game average in a season? Hint: While the selfish lummox was clogging up passing lanes in order to beef up his steal stats, the man he was covering was in the corner burying jumpers and leading his team to a thing called the "playoffs.".

29) Which player had the highest career scoring average—Larry Bird, Adrian Dantley, Charles Barkley, or Rick Barry? Editor's note: The most popular answer is "who gives a shit?"

30) Name the four NBA ball hogs who have displayed their greed by scoring over 70 points in what was once considered a team game.

ANSWERS

BASKETBALL

25) Don Nelson—Milwaukee Bucks in 1983

26) Don Nelson has won 0.0000 titles. This figure, when rounded up and multiplied by 2 million, indicates just how much he sucks.

27) Bill Fitch had a record of 999-1157 and would like to thank the L.A. Clippers for fouling up his resume.

28) Alvin Robertson with 3.67 steals/game.

29) Larry Bird with a 24.3 avg.

30) Wilt Chamberlain hogged it for 100 points in 1962 in a game of 1 on 5 (he also scored 78, 73, 73, 72 and 70 until finally the other teams caught on that Wilt was the go-to guy on offense), David Thompson scored 73 in 1978, Elgin Baylor scored 71 in 1960 and David Robinson refused to pass for 71 in 1994.

SCORE_____

DIVISION 1 COLLEGE BASKETBALL

1) Since the NBA Lottery began in 1985, which collection of buildings for drinking and screwing (i.e. which college) has had the most players selected with the number one pick? Hint: The men are currently putting their hard earned education to work bouncing leather balls and high fiving grown men in the NBA.

2) Which current NBA star has the NCAA record for highest assist average in a season with 13.3? (He's also adept at passing off blame every time he screws up, which happens to be quite often.)

3) Who is the only player to block 200 shots (that weren't going in anyway) in a season? Hint: His diet consists of leather, shit and a steady dose of losses that are mainly his fault.

4) Name the only three players to lead the nation in ball hogging and camping out underneath the rim (scoring and rebounding) in the same season.

5) Six players have committed the mortal sin of greed by scoring over 3,000 points in a NCAA career while their teammates stood around and watched. Who are they?

ANSWERS

COLLEGE BASKETBALL

1) Georgetown—Allen Iverson and Patrick Ewing

2) Avery Johnson—the high pitched fairy out of Cameron/Southern.

3) David Robinson for Navy in 1986. Several blocks went right over the deck and landed in the ocean.

4) Hank Gathers 1989, Kurt Thomas 1995 and Xavier McDaniel 1985

5) Pete Maravich (LSU), Freeman Williams (Portland St.), Lionel Simmons (LaSalle), Alphonzo Ford (Miss. Valley St.), Harry Kelly (Texas Southern) and Hersey Hawkins (Bradley).

SCORE_____

COLLEGE BASKETBALL

6) Giving new meaning to the term selfishness, name the aforementioned 3,000 point scorer who did it in only three seasons. Hints: In his junior year he attempted his first pass. It went in.

7) Who is the only gawky looking bastard to pull his shorts up to his neck and score 3,000 points and grab 1,000 rebounds from his own bricked shots in a career?

8) If you can name the only player to score 2,000 points and grab 2,000 rebounds in a career, then I feel completely sorry for you.

9) When Pete Maravich scored a then record 69 points in a game he pissed off his teammates, pleased Satan and broke the record set the previous year by what future NBA self-gloating shithead?

10) Who broke several commandments, as well as Pete Maravich's NCAA record for avarice in 1991 by scoring 72 points?

11) Who twice wore the other team's colors so he could make a record 13 steals in a NCAA game? Hint: His signature move after stealing a pass is to give it right back via the air ball or the muffed dribble between the legs.

ANSWERS

COLLEGE BASKETBALL

6) Pete Maravich

7) Lionel Simmons of Lasalle.

8) Joe Holup of George Washington.

9) Calvin Murphy who did it for Niagara, because he couldn't get into a real school.

10) Kevin Bradshaw of US Int'l.

11) Mookie Blaylock in 1987-88 against two schools you never heard of.

SCORE_____

COLLEGE BASKETBALL

12) Which NCAA champ actually sucked (had the most losses ever by a champion in one season)? Hint: They play in the Midwest where life consists of shooting hoops and drinking an all-natural version of light block milk by sucking a cow's udder during a solar eclipse.

13) Name the four schools that went undefeated en route to winning the NCAA championship. Hint: They won all their games and never lost all season. The players later proceeded out into the real world and secured jobs as fry cooks in a burger shack.

14) Name the two teams involved in the NCAA title game that resulted in a complete waste of beer, drugs and a Monday night (30 point lopsided yawner—the largest deficit all time).

15) Who is the last crybaby to be named Most Outstanding Player of the NCAA tournament despite playing for the losing squad?

16) Name the current NBA player who holds the career record for most points in the NCAA tourney. Hint: He hit one clutch shot in college and zero in the pros. His signature move is to glare at the wide open guy in the corner as he tosses up a one-handed leaning cinder block whilst flipping the coach the bird with his free hand. On other days his attitude is not so good.

ANSWERS

COLLEGE BASKETBALL

12) In 1988 Kansas lost a pathetic 11 games and were invited to the tournament based solely on the size of their cheerleaders breasts.

13) Indiana (1976), UCLA (1964, 1967, 1972, 1973), San Francisco (1956) and North Carolina (1957).

14) UNLV beat Duke in 1990 by a score of 103—73. When asked to add these two figures a UNLV player said it equals "a lot of blue and red chips."

15) Hakeem Olajuwon in 1983 for Houston University.

16) Christian Laettner with 407 points.

SCORE_____

COLLEGE BASKETBALL

---

17) Name the eight men to be named College Player of the Year with all the cellophane still on their study materials, and then go on to win NBA MVP while living in a mansion with twelve empty bookcases.

18) Who are the two St. John's players to be named Player of the Year back to back in 1985-86? Hint: One was pigment-impaired.

19) Despite the public's desire to have him castrated and lynched, name the only active coach to have a winning percentage over .800 and a total of under 100 career losses (minimum 5 years coaching at Division 1)?

20) Can you name the last two schools to win the NCAA title despite actually having shitty teams (entering the tourney unranked)?

21) Who am I? I was named Most Outstanding Player of the tourney, despite making only eight field goals in the Final Four. I did however, block a record 15 shots and haul down 18 rebounds. I am also one of the ugliest men on the planet. My hobbies are screaming at refs because I can't make a single shot, and fouling out in the first quarter.

ANSWERS

COLLEGE BASKETBALL

17) Larry Bird, Bill Walton, Kareem Abdul Jabbar, Oscar Robertson, Bill Russell, David Robinson, Michael Jordan and Shaquille O'Neal.

18) Chris Mullin and Walter Berry. Berry had a great NBA career—scoring 4 points, grabbing half a board and committing 2,300 fouls.

19) Roy Williams of Kansas.

20) Kansas in 1988 and Villanova in 1985.

21) Patrick Ewing did it in 1984. He has been ugly since 1964.

SCORE_____

COLLEGE BASKETBALL

22) Cast your vote for the collegiate star who averaged a record 43.5 points per game in the Final Four and was named Most Outstanding Player despite having played on the losing side. Hint: Despite being retired he got his ass whupped again in 2000.

23) Who am I? I also lost in the final game of the tourney and shot a paltry 34% in the Final Four for Seattle. I was named Most Outstanding player based on my 41 assists and 24 points/game. As a pro I continued to refuse sharing the ball with my teammates. My hobbies are hiking, skiing and slapping media people in the face.

24) Nine of the top ten schools in all time winning percentage have had basketball programs in existence for over 75 years. The other school has had a hoop program for less than 45 years. Name the school. Hint: Books were introduced on the campus in 1998. Writing utensils soon followed.

25) Only two players have exposed their sweaty underarms in order to stink up the court and lead the nation in blocked shots more than once. Who are these two stench-ridden genetic mutations?

26) Which collection of gloryhounds was so desperate to be recognized, they stayed down one end of the court the entire season in order to post the highest team scoring average of all time? Hint: It obviously didn't work because I never heard of these clowns before.

ANSWERS

COLLEGE BASKETBALL

22) Bill Bradley for Princeton in 1965.

23) Elgin Baylor in 1958 for Seattle University.

24) Casino University (UNLV)

25) David Robinson and Keith Closs

26) Loyola, California in 1990 with a 122.4 pts per game avg.

SCORE_____

COLLEGE BASKETBALL

27) Can you name the city which has hosted the most Final Four tourneys? Hint: Dullsville, U.S.A. Typical day: Wake up, spread manure and then go to bed.

28) Name the only two guards to amass over 1,000 assists in their college careers. Hint: Their NBA careers could best be described by watching shit calcify into hard white chunks.

29) Which of the following lazy NBA millionaires never led the NCAA in rebounding? David Robinson, Shaquille O'Neal, Akeem "The Wet Dream" Olajuwon, Alonzo Mourning. Hint: His signature move is to lay 20 up-fakes while the defender yawns and waits for the ball to appear, so he can slap it back in the stiff's face. He has a great touch around the basket as almost all his shots end up touching some portion of the basket assembly; i.e. rim, basket, net, support, base or shot clock.

30) When is the last time the voters weren't completely cocked when they filled out their ballots? (What eventual NCAA Champ was the last one to enter the tourney ranked number one?)

ANSWERS

COLLEGE BASKETBALL

27) Kansas City (Municipal Auditorium) Halftime entertainment: Put 30 cents in a machine and a 12 oz. can of liquid miraculously appears out of nowhere.

28) Chris Corchiani and Bobby Hurley

29) Alonzo Mourning

30) The 1995 UCLA Bruins

SCORE_____

THE SARCASTIC SPORTS TRIVIA BOOK

HOCKEY

---

1) Who is the only coach to go completely bald as a result of three straight sweeps in the Cup Finals? Hint: He had 432 wispy hairs clinging for dear life when this book went to print.

2) Because hockey writers spend most of the game drinking, eating cheese snacks and getting arrested, when it comes time to vote for awards most of them need a game program just to come up with a guy's name. This has resulted in a total of four Conn Smythe Trophy winners (MVP of the Finals, for all you folks with teeth) who did not play for the winning team. Who were these players?

3) Which two teams have the best winning percentage (i.e. appearances vs. Cups won—minimum of two) in the Cup Finals?

4) Name the Boston Bruin who holds the record for most points in a playoff series with 19. Hint: He's as bald as a walnut, but nobody knew because his helmet covered up his shiny pock-marked dome.

5) Which ingrate has scored the most goals (12) in a playoff series? Hints: He loved to park his little Finnish ass in the slot so he could fire the puck and then race over to the bench before any shit went down. His last name translated means "petrified."

ANSWERS

HOCKEY

1) Scotty Bowman with St. Louis in 1968—1970.

2) Roger Crozier (1966), Glenn Hall (1968), Reggie Leach (1976) and Ron Hextall (1987).

3) Pittsburgh Penguins also known as the "Lemieux's" (2 for 2) and the original Ottawa Senators (4 for 4). The current Ottawa Senators are 0 for 0 and will remain so for decades as they are haunted by the ghost of Alexi Yashin.

4) Rick Middleton had 19 points and 2,398 hair plug transplants vs. Buffalo in 1983.

5) Jari Kurri with 12 goals vs. Chicago in 1985. He later went out for beers with his teammates and inquired "who the hell are these guys?"

SCORE_____

HOCKEY

6) Which of the following was never a nickname of Montreal: Wanderers, Shamrocks, AAA, or Blueshirts?

7) Who is the last player other than Jagr, Lemieux or Gretzky to win the scoring title? Hint: You have to go back to 1980 to come up with the name of the dainty center man who somehow accomplished this despite cowering in fear at the red line the majority of his career.

8) Which five net hogs reached the 500 goal plateau the fastest by firing shot after shot on a well covered net while wide open guys lost their voices screaming "pass the frigging puck just once you greedy nipplehead!"

9) Which slow poke took 1,370 games to reach the 500 goal plateau, the last one coming on an empty netter potted from the seat of a wheelchair as Molson Ale and Viagra were intravenously pumped into his orifice?

10) Who is the last puck hog to lead the league in scoring with more total goals than assists? Hint: He knocked his own teeth out because they were interfering with the flow of beer.

11) Who are the three other net hangers to lead the league in scoring with more goals than assists? Hint: Occasionally they would pick up an accidental assist and then would smash their stick over the boards in disgust.

ANSWERS

HOCKEY

6) Blueshirts

7) Marcel Dionne led the league with 53 goals, 84 assists and also chickened out of eight fights.

8) Wayne Gretzky, Mike Bossy, Mario Lemieux, Brett Hull and Phil Esposito.

9) John Bucyk

10) Bobby Hull in 1966 with 56 goals and 43 other shots (assists) that were tipped home by teammates as Bobby screamed, "It's going in, don't touch it you asshole!"

11) Gordie Howe in 1952, '53, Jean Beliveau 1956 and Bernie Geoffrion 1961.

SCORE_____

HOCKEY

---

12) Who led the league in total goals a record seven times before finally realizing he had teammates? He is currently a G.M. known for his ability to mastermind a franchise into the throes of bankruptcy while his own wallet remains as fat as ever.

13) Name the selfish bastard who didn't meet his goalie until his career was over, because he was down the other end leading the league in goals six straight years. Hint: He has a son who plays in the league and who coincidentally shares his Dad's belief that passing is a crime that should be punishable by death.

14) Name the six players with tunnel vision who have scored 75 or more goals in a season by spending the previous off-season consuming themselves with greed.

15) The top 13 scoring seasons in NHL history all belong to Gretzky and Lemieux, because they practiced hockey while the other players drank beers and then sped around Canada half in the wrapper. Which tee-totaling eunuch finally breaks their hold on these marks with the 14th best season ever (155 points)?

16) Wayne Gretzky holds nine of the top 11 scoring season marks in history. How many of these were done in Edmonton and how many while sleeping with Janet Jones (Los Angeles)?

ANSWERS

HOCKEY

12) Bobby Hull committed the sin 7 times and is considered a shoo-in for hell.

13) Phil Esposito did it 6 years in a row by parking his hairy Ginzo ass out in front of the net 60 minutes a night.

14) Phil Esposito (76 goals), Teemu Selanne (76), Alex Mogilny (76), Mario Lemieux (85), Brett Hull (86), and Wayne Gretzky (92).

15) Steve Yzerman in 1988-89 with 65 goals and 90 assists.

16) Gretzky won 7 scoring titles with Edmonton and only two with L.A. proving that sex is a deterrent to athletics.

SCORE_____

HOCKEY

---

17) Name the inept coach who hung around so long he now has the most all-time coaching victories without a Stanley Cup. His pre-game ritual was to glance at the blackboard and then at his players with a look of horror on his face.

18) Who was the last left winger to win the league MVP? Hints: He and his pet piranha combined for 32 teeth. He once pummeled a statistician for crediting him with multiple assists.

19) Because right wingers would rather suck face with an Ebola monkey than muck in the corner and because they rarely show up in big games, only three right wingers have won league MVP since 1965. Each of these years the voters had to check into rehab for crack abuse. Name these overrated yellow-bellied right wingers. Hint: Each has a faggy first name and long hair to match.

20) Name the only three Rookie of the Year winners to care so little about others that they scored over 50 goals in their inaugural season. Hint: Inaugural means first.

21) Who are the three defensemen to win the Norris Trophy with two different clubs? The term defensemen is used very lightly, since in order to win the Norris, you have to tell your abused goalie "see you in three hours" and go park your ass in front of the opponents net for the night collecting points and scalping opponents with the blade of your stick.

ANSWERS

HOCKEY

17) Billy Reay who coached Toronto and Chicago to 599 meaningless hollow victories.

18) Bobby Hull

19) Guy Lafleur 1977-78, Brett Hull 1991 and Jaromir Jagr 1999.

20) Mike Bossy 1978, Joe Nieuwendyk 1988 and Teemu Selanne 1993.

21) Paul Coffey—Edmonton and Detroit, Chris Chelios—Montreal and Chicago, and Doug Harvey—Montreal and N.Y. Rangers.

SCORE_____

HOCKEY

22) Name the player who immediately grasped the concept of hunning it by scoring the most points ever by a Rookie of the Year winner. His signature move is to hang around the net adding up his points while simultaneously watching his teammates get the snot beat out of them by the other team, the refs and several hundred rabid drunken fans.

23) Name the seven players who have won three or more league MVP awards. Several won it because they stood out amongst really sucky teammates.

24) Who is the only goalie to win multiple MVP awards? Hint: He also has a gold medal, a Porsche and an original copy of Marx's Communist Manifesto.

25) The toothless mutant who has the all-time record for most penalties in a game (10) spent most of his career behind bars or playing in Canada. Name this scarred, pus-infected lunatic. Hint: His signature move was to lug the puck up to center ice and then fire it at the opposing teams' bench in an effort to kill someone. His pinpoint accuracy caused Canadian health insurance rates to skyrocket.

26) Five egocentric players have led the league in scoring three or more consecutive years with Satan riding atop their left shoulder. Who are these future visitors to HADES?

ANSWERS

HOCKEY

22) Teemu Selanne in 1993 with 132 points. Selanne has now been the answer to three questions. Only a total idiot would get all three wrong.

23) Wayne Gretzky, Gordie Howe, Bobby Orr, Howie Morenz, Mario Lemieux, Eddie Shore and Bobby Clarke.

24) Dominik Hasek in 1997 and 1998 despite a goaltending style that would run most guys out of the league in a day.

25) Chris Nilan on 3/31/91 according to police records.

26) Gordie Howe 1951-1954, Phil Esposito 1971-74, Guy Lafleur 1976-78, Wayne Gretzky 1981-87 and Jagr 98-00

SCORE_____

HOCKEY

---

27) Who are the only three players in history to satisfy the lust of others by dishing 100 or more assists in one season to their begging drooling linemates?

28) Which goalie retired in 1997 with the highest winning percentage all time (minimum 300 victories)? Hint: Great team, shitty goalie.

29) Who is the only Pittsburgh Penguin to win the Norris Trophy? He thought the trophy was named after Chuck Norris so he spent most of the season kicking people in the face with the blades of his skates.

30) Name the Selke Award winner (best defensive forward) who once scored 56 goals in a season and also found time to illegally fondle underage girls' breasts?

ANSWERS

HOCKEY

27) Bobby Orr, Wayne Gretzky and Mario Lemieux.

28) Andy Moog, who despite flopping around so much the holes in his mask weren't lined up with his eyes half the time, still was able to win because Messier and Gretzky were good enough to keep the puck far away from this untalented nipplebrain.

29) Randy Carlyle in 1981.

30) Sergei Federov in 1994.

SCORE_____

BASEBALL

---

1) After the Yankees 25 corporate sponsored World Series victories, which two franchises have purchased nine titles?

2) After losing two straight World Series games to Atlanta in 1996, the Yankees were shown stacks of money and then won the next four and then swept the Braves in the 1999 World Series. Name the other joke of a franchise that the Yankees have a current eight game winning streak against in World Series play.

3) Which franchise has won the fewest games in World Series play (minimum one appearance)? Hint: The franchise was created to hide illegal cash transactions (pronounced "founded") by a gap-toothed lard ass who is adored by millions of overweight, malnourished gluttons.

4) Which three players have won multiple World Series MVP's? Hint: One is a cocky gap-toothed jackass and the other two would have loved to cram a fastball down his trachea.

5) Name the unheralded manager of the 1983 World Champion Baltimore Orioles. Hint: He is now an old fart who enjoys staring at old team photos while a nurse tries to find one of his veins.

ANSWERS

BASEBALL

1) Philadelphia—Oakland Athletics and the St. Louis Cardinals.

2) The last two times the Yankees faced the Chicago Cubs (1932 and 1938) they swept the series.

3) San Diego has appeared twice and won a total of one measly rotten game. Ray Kroc of Shit was the owner. The game is still under protest as officials try to figure out how San Diego could have possibly won a game.

4) Sandy Koufax, Bob Gibson and Reggie "me, me, me, me, me, me, me, me, me, me, me" Jackson.

5) Joe Altobelli. Note: Even Joe Altobelli got this one wrong by guessing Earl Weaver.

SCORE_____

BASEBALL

6) What is the only position on the diamond not represented by a World Series MVP? Several people have replied DH, despite the fact that DH is not a position on the diamond. They then proceed to throw out pinch hitter and runner at which point I walk away and vow never to speak again.

7) The only 2B to be voted the World Series MVP is also the only guy to win it despite playing for the losers. Coincidentally he played for N.Y., where most of the voters live so they can be close to the players who bribe them. Who is this undeserving jackoff?

8) Which franchise has the best winning percentage (appearances vs. Series won) in World Series play amongst those with at least five appearances? Hint: The billionaire owner recently went on a spending spree that raised the payroll to $836.89.

9) Which two pathetic franchises have the worst percentage of World Series won amongst those with at least five appearances?

10) Name the only babysitter (baseball manager) to sweep a World Series and then be bitchslapped 4-0 the following year by a manager who exposed him for the overrated nitwit that he really is. Hint: His signature move is to take a simple game and turn it into a science project. For example, if he is leading 8-0 in the ninth inning and his starter is breezing along with a two hitter, this dimwitted mulyak will yank his ass off the mound and bring in fifteen clowns from the bullpen to "nail" down the win. He will then hold a press conference to discuss his brilliant decision to bring in the lefty to face a lefty with two outs in the

ninth, two strikes on the hitter and the remainder of the opposing team already naked and showering.

11) Which franchise has used its incredibly high tax bracket, along with a staff of crooked accountants, in order to cook the books en route to winning the most National League pennants?

ANSWERS

BASEBALL

6) Center field

7) Bobby Richardson for the Yankees in 1960, His Series stats—7 punch and judy hits, 12 easy putouts that could have been made by a monkey on crack and 4 checks written out to the Associated Press.

8) Pittsburgh Pirates with 5 wins in 7 appearances.

9) The Philadelphia Phillies and the Chicago Cubs (.200).

10) Tony Larussa in 1989 and 1990 with the Oakland A's. He beat the Giants in 1989 because he focused on winning whereas most people were busy that weekend trying to save earthquake victims, then the following year the Reds spanked his ass 4-0.

11) L.A. Dodgers

SCORE_____

INTERMISSION

BASEBALL

---

12) Name the only two San Diego Padres to win a NL batting title. Growing up, one honed his swing with a bat and ball, the other with a broken beer bottle and innocent peoples' heads.

13) Which player said "screw the team" as he set the record for the most consecutive NL batting titles with six? His signature move was to ground out, then run up to the press box and choke the scorer until it was recorded as a hit.

14) Name the four other self-indulgent major leaguers to win four or more consecutive batting titles by placing their personal goals in the forefront. Hint: Three of the men were known to run to first base clutching a calculator. The fourth played in the early days and was forced to lug a wooden abacus.

15) Who is the only AL player to win more than one batting title in the 90's? Hint: His nose is so big he can stuff a baseball in each nostril and still have room for his fat stubby fingers.

16) The only batting titlist with an asterisk next to his name won it in the AL in 1961. What is an asterisk and why is there an asterisk? Hint: His last name is the only reason I wrote this book.

17) Speaking of fatties, name the last Pittsburgh Pirate to lead the NL in homers by generating power from his cellulite-ridden ass cheeks and then by following through with really loud anal eructations.

ANSWERS

BASEBALL

12) Tony Gwynn in 1987-89 and 1994-97 and Gary Sheffield in 1992.

13) Rogers Hornsby with six from 1920 to 1925.

14) Tony Gwynn, Wade Boggs, Rod Carew and Honus Wagner

15) Edgar Martinez in 1992 and '95. Nostril circumference 4.6 inches, Ego: Infinite, Ass hairs: 2,389 , Wallet: 10 pounds.

16) Norm Cash who hit .361, but later cowardly admitted to corking his bat after all his paychecks had cleared. He played 16 other seasons and never hit higher than .286 (* = asterisk—a star-shaped figure used in print to indicate an omission, a footnote or some record that is tainted because the holder is either a coward, a liar or a bat corking asshole.)

17) Willie Stargell in 1971 with 48 homers and 316 liters of homemade lethal gas.

SCORE_____

BASEBALL

---

18) The only active player in 2000 to have three RBI titles to his name has also played for three different teams, because he is a jackass who would rip my nuts off if he saw this. Name this madman.

19) If you can name the four Triple Crown winners in the 1930's, then it's time to pull the plug on the life support.

20) Who holds the record for most consecutive stolen base titles with eight? Hint: He could move his legs back and forth really fast.

21) Of all the players to go 30/30 (30 steals—30 homers) only one has ever stolen 50 bases in that season. He did it in only 129 games and has been injured through most of his career. Who is this brittle waste of a major league roster spot? Hint: His most recent injury was a slipped disk suffered when he bent over to moon fans at a charity event.

22) Which player had the longest hitting streak in the 1990's? Hint: He has a brother who plays in the majors and an aunt who doesn't.

ANSWERS

BASEBALL

18) Albert Belle (Chicago (AL), Cleveland and Baltimore)

19) Jimmie Foxx, Lou Gehrig, Chuck Klein, and Joe Medwick

20) Luis Aparicio with 8.

21) Eric Davis for the Reds.

22) Vladimir Guerrero with 31 consecutive games. This means that Dimaggio's streak is either truly amazing or today's players truly suck or both.

SCORE_____

BASEBALL

---

23) Name the only player with three hitting streaks of 30 or more games in his career. Hint: His signature move was to swing for the fences when the situation was screaming BUNT. His hobbies include, in order: drinking, gay bashing, assault and battery, and blacking out minutes before game time.

24) Since 1970 only 4 pitchers have won the pitching Triple Crown. Who are they? Hint: A couple of real assholes in this group.

25) Who are the only two relief pitchers to amass over 400 saves? Hint: One is a lefty, the other eats with his right, picks cheese from his ass with his left and skillfully flips fans off with both.

26) Amongst the top 25 home run hitters of all time, which five have abused steroids the most and therefore have the best Home Run Per At Bat Ratios? Hint: Three are still on 'roids, one is on Viagra and one is buried under six feet of topsoil.

27) Name the last two unwanted migrants to lead the AL in homers and then later in their career lead the NL in homers because neither league bothers to drug test these phony thugs.

ANSWERS

BASEBALL

23) Ty Cobb had streaks that lasted 34, 35 and 40 games. He also had a racial streak that lasted his entire life.

24) Steve Carlton ignored the media and won it in 1972, Dwight Gooden snorted his way to it in 1985, Roger Clemens did it in 1997-98 because assholes finish first and Pedro Martinez somehow did it in 1999 while talking to the media, abstaining from coke and behaving like a nice guy.

25) John Franco and Lee Smith

26) Mark McGwire (with the help of a bunch of drugs), Babe Ruth, Harmon Killebrew, Ted Williams and Jose Canseco

27) Mark McGwire (A's and on drugs with the Cardinals) and Fred McGriff (Blue Jays and Padres)

SCORE_____

BASEBALL

---

28) Only two pitchers in the top 10 all time winning percentage list have accumulated over 300 victories. Hint: They played back when gloves weren't used, bats were made out of tofu and simple addition was typically off by several hundred figures.

29) Since 1950, four players have destroyed team chemistry (accumulated 400 total bases in a single season) by constantly swinging for the fences with the hit and run play on. Name these rapacious maggots.

30) Name the first and last players to hit four home runs in a game during the 20th century. Hint: One is a legend and the other is a bat-corking philanderer.

ANSWERS

BASEBALL

28) Christy Mathewson and Lefty Grove

29) Hank Aaron -1959, Jim Rice -1978, Larry Walker -1997, Sammy Sosa -1998 and Todd Helton -2000. With the exception of Rice, who happened to play in a park the size of a sandbox, each of the teams that housed these selfish wretches were so far out of first place they were selling off talent by early May.

30) Lou Gehrig (Yankees) and Mark Whiten (Cardinals). What a great way to start the century and what a shitty way to end it.

SCORE_____

FOOTBALL

---

1) Name the first two receivers to each have 1,000 yards receiving for the same team in the same season despite having a sucky quarterback short arming wobbly spirals way over their heads into the photographers' area.

2) Name the three wide receivers who won Super Bowl MVP, then headed off on a drunken spree in Orlando, stumbling around and puking on all the rides.

3) A total of five coaches have employed their inept talents to lose a total of 19 Super Bowls. Who are these men? Hints: Four have lost four apiece and one lost three. Two are legally retarded. All five suck.

4) What is the only team that has made more than one appearance in the Super Bowl and is undefeated in those appearances? Hint: They consistently seem to make the Super Bowl in years when the AFC sends some lame ass pack of befuddled morons as its' representative.

5) Because their running backs were gimpy, dink toed, no-talent bums in dire need of knee surgery, two quarterbacks were forced to suffer massive beatings while passing for over 1,000 career yards in their Super Bowl appearances. Who are these two unfortunate men?

ANSWERS

FOOTBALL

1) Herman Moore and Brett Perriman for Detroit. (Scott Mitchell was the sucky QB.)

2) Jerry Rice 1989, Fred Belitnikof '77 and Lynn Swann '76.

3) Don Shula, Dan Reeves, Bud Grant and Marv Levy all lost 4. Tom Landry lost 3. How pathetic.

4) S.F. 49ers (too many years to mention—look up the years yourself).

5) John Elway and Joe Montana

SCORE_____

FOOTBALL

---

6) Who is the only quarterback to lead the league in passing four consecutive years while his millionaire running back screamed, "Trade me you fascist bastards!!!" in the backfield?

7) The NFC did not see a 100 reception season by a wide receiver until 1984. Who finally did it by catching 106 one yard dumpoffs? Hint: His signature move was to take one step over the line, catch the ball and then roll up in a ball screaming "please don't hit me—I have a headache."

8) You're a crusty old bat with tubes up your nose if you know the name of the first AFC receiver to catch 100 passes in 1961. Hint: His signature move was to completely burn the slow assed redneck cornerback trying to cover him and then turn to watch his racist quarterback toss it to an ineligible white receiver for a gain of minus 20.

9) Who won more AFC rushing titles, Franco "I'm going out of bounds so you can't hit me" Harris or Larry "mo-hair chest" Csonka?

10) Who is the only player in history to lead both conferences in rushing? Hint: He's an ass who later got a broadcasting job despite possessing the oratory skills of a lispy drunk on ecstasy.

ANSWERS

FOOTBALL

6) Steve Young from 1991—1994. The back was Ricky Watters who later was furloughed to the Seattle Seahawks who felt that the Dome noise would make it difficult for Ricky to be heard. They were wrong.

7) Art Monk. Monk celebrated by heading straight to the showers and calling it a season.

8) Lionel Taylor of Denver with 100. Taylor actually caught only 50 balls but because of the confusion associated with a new idea called "instant replay" he was credited with 100. His team was constantly criticized as being too repetitive.

9) They each tied with zero. Franco did lead the league in Hard Hits Avoided every year that he "played."

10) Eric Dick(head)erson. Eric is currently busy assaulting America's eardrums by performing John Thompson impersonations on Monday Night Football.

SCORE_____

FOOTBALL

---

11) Name the four rushers who have gained over 2,000 yards in a season and which one had the best yards per carry average in that season? Useless hint: None are white, but one most likely killed some white people.

12) Who came out of the final game of the season just 66 yards short of the 2,000 yard barrier in the early 1980's because the team stat guy sucked at addition? Hint: His signature move was to ignore the play called in the huddle and just run right up the middle stiff arming helpless linemen and stepping on the empty head of any poor cornerback who got in his way.

13) Who are the last five non-wussies (non-kickers) to put on a normal looking football helmet and lead their conference in scoring?

14) Name the five running backs to rush for 20 or more TD's in a season. Hint: One of the selfish bastard's best moves was to mope out of the huddle acting all pissed off about the play call; then when his quarterback held the ball up to look for a receiver this prick would pull it out of his hand and run it in for the score.

15) Who am I? I played running back in the NFC (1970's) and once had a season with over twenty TD's by rushing for thirteen and catching nine passes for touchdowns. I led the NFC in catches one year. Towards the end of my career my ass bone hurt and I sucked real bad.

ANSWERS

FOOTBALL

11) O.J. Simpson 1973, Eric Dickerson 1984, Barry Sanders 1997, Terrell Davis 1998. Barry Sanders had the best average with 6.1 yards per carry. O.J. had the best criminal mind. Dickheaderson was the quietest on the sidelines. Unfortunately this no longer holds true.

12) Earl Campbell for Houston in 1980. I have no bad words for Earl Campbell.....yet.

13) Jerry Rice, Emmitt Smith, Marcus Allen, Wendell Tyler and Marshall Faulk.

14) John Riggins, E(n)mmitt(y) Smith, Terrell Davis, Terry Allen and Joe Morris.

15) Chuck Foreman

SCORE_____

FOOTBALL

16) Senility is just around the corner if you can remember the first man in NFL history to rush for over 1,000 yards. Hint: He played back when plays were drawn up on papyrus and then brought into the huddle via camel by a running back wearing sandals and a tunic.

17) Amongst tight ends, who has caught the most passes in Super Bowl history? Hint: He often got open by completely fouling up his blocking assignment, then drifting into the open field to catch the ball just as his QB was being hospitalized by a steroid crazed lineman.

18) Name the franchise that has won the most postseason games. Hint: The franchise is currently owned by an arrogant, camera-mugging millionaire who, rather than spend $75.43 on a cleaning, prefers to allow his teeth to rot a disgusting shade of yellow.

19) Name the eight receivers who have caught over 800 passes in their NFL careers. If you're real bored, name the 3,425 who haven't. Then name the 323,675,888 people who never played in the NFL.

20) In the top ten all time passing yardage leaders only two have completed over 60% of their attempts. Quick math tells me that 40% of the time they accomplished absolutely nothing. Who are these mediocre talents?

ANSWERS

FOOTBALL

16) Beattie Feathers for the Chicago Bears in 1934 with 1,004 yards.

17) Jay Novacek of the Cowboys with 17 catches.

18) Dallas Cowboys with 32. The owner is Jerry Jones. Jerry's dentist is Dr. Morris who claims he hasn't seen Jerry in 41 years.

19) Chris Carter, Jerry Rice, Art Monk, Andre Reed, Steve Largent, Henry Ellard, Irving Fryar and Tim Brown.

20) Jim Kelly of the Bills and Joe Montana of the 49er's.

SCORE_____

FOOTBALL

21) Despite deserving neither, who is the last "man" to win the Heisman Trophy and be selected number one in the NFL draft? Hints: His passes are often shot down by skeet shooters in the stands who mistake his wobbly parabolic throws for targets. He has been injured several times when an opposing player ran up and tackled him. A recent MRI revealed that he has no heart whatsoever and his brain is the exact same size as one of his testicles.

22) Who was the last defensive player to be named NFL MVP? Hint: He celebrated the award by using the sharp end of the trophy to slice up an eight ball of coke. The trophy was then hollowed out and converted to a hash bong. The Smithsonian declined an offer to house the precious keepsake. VH1 has expressed interest in running his life story in an episode of Behind The Music, but he needs to put out a song first.

23) Name the only player to be named AP Player of the Year three times.

24) Prior to 1999 only one of the six divisions in the NFL has never had a 100 reception receiver. Name it. Hint: A brain dead meteorologist could figure this one out.

25) A total of only two AFC players have caught over 110 passes in a season, because AFC teams believe in running smack dab into a pile of steroid abused behemoths in the middle of a frigging blizzard. Who are the two?

ANSWERS

FOOTBALL

21) Vinnie Testaverde of Miami University in 1987.

22) Lawrence Taylor in 1986 for the Giants.

23) Earl Campbell of Houston. At his retirement press conference Earl said, "I wish there was some way I could thank the fans." Note to Earl: It's called winning a Super Bowl you thunder thighed mulyak.

24) The AFC East. Reason: The litany of wussy QB's who blow on their hands and whimper, "It's too cold to pass, let's punt and get over to those frigging sideline heaters."

25) Jimmy Smith of Jacksonville in 1999 and Marvin Harrison in 1999.

SCORE_____

FOOTBALL

---

26) Name the six white backfield members (i.e. Quarterbacks) who passed for 35 or more touchdowns in a season, because they lacked the balls to run it in themselves.

27) The last time a St Louis—Arizona Cardinal won a rushing title was in 1975. He was white, leading me to believe blacks weren't allowed in St. Louis in 1975. Who was this one hit wonder?

28) Despite a crummy attitude, who was the first receiver in NFL history to put together back to back 100 illegal push-offs (receptions) seasons? Hint: The pompous asshole's career came to a tragic end when he suffered major inflammation to his ego.

29) Which category has a Pittsburgh Steeler never led the league in? Rushing, Passing, Cheap shots to the nuts, DUI convictions, drug busts or Receptions. Hint: Bam Morris once played for the Steelers.

30) Who are the only two running backs in NFL history to rush and receive for over 1,000 yards in a season? Hint: Each played on high powered offenses which allowed these two pipsqueaks to sneak around undetected by defenses that were busy covering players with talent. If either of these two played back in the 1950's and 60's the question would read "Name the only two men to be killed on their first NFL carry from scrimmage." Their career stats would read: Seconds Played—5, Carries—1, Fumbles—1, Yards Gained—Minus 19, Contributions to the game—His death led to the abolition of midgets and circus freaks in the NFL.

ANSWERS

FOOTBALL

26) Dan Marino (48 TD's), Brett Favre (39), Kurt Warner (40), Y.A. Tittle (36), Steve Young (36) and George Blanda (36).

27) Jim Otis with 1,076 yards.

28) Sterling Sharpe in 1992 and '93

29) Receptions

30) Roger Craig and Marshall Faulk

SCORE_____

DIVISION 1 COLLEGE FOOTBALL

1) Which school has been ranked number one in the final polls a record eight times? The average grade point of the numbskulled players is coincidentally also one after rounding the number up and cubing it.

2) Which school has placed academics in the background so it could get in the Final Top 20 a record 46 times? Hint: A UFO sighting was reported last fall but it turned out to be an opened textbook.

3) Which school's alumni has orally pleasured the most TV execs (which school has appeared in the most bowls)? Hint: Not to be confused with Miami, the school that has packed and smoked the most bowls.

4) Of the major corporate sponsored bowls—the Orange Bowl, Fiesta Bowl, Sugar Bowl, Cotton Bowl and the Rose Bowl, which one has been won a record 11 times by rapists and thieves?

5) Only one of the major bowls has been won three consecutive years by the same team. Name the bowl and the school. (No hint on this one as I have no idea myself. The answer at the back of the book is a wild guess. If you would like to return this question for a refund please cut it out and mail it back to the publisher. Please allow 10 -12 years for delivery.)

ANSWERS

COLLEGE FOOTBALL

1) Notre Dame

2) Michigan

3) Alabama with 49.

4) Oklahoma has traveled down to Florida and won the Orange Bowl 11 times. Incidentally, homicides went up 50% over those weekends. Coach Bud Wilkinson declined comment. Barry Switzer said (as he loaded shotguns into his briefcase at the airport lounge), "I had nothing to do with it since I've never been there or any other island in the Pacific for that matter."

5) Alabama won the Sugar Bowl from 1978 thru 1980 with college students ranging in age from 18 to 35.

SCORE_____

DIVISION 1 COLLEGE FOOTBALL

6) Since 1970 when the NCAA went to a yards per game criteria for the rushing title, who are the only four ballhogs to lead the nation with an average of over 200 yards per game? Hint: One player spent his college years protesting for black civil rights—he later starred in TV cop shows where young blacks were innocently shot up in the streets.

7) Since 1970, who are the five rushers to lead the nation in yards/game in consecutive years? Hint: They rewarded their linemen with one thousand dollar gift certificates for pharmaceuticals. The linemen proceeded to climb through the drive thru window of the nearest Walgreens and wolf down every capsule in sight.

8) Name the pathetic football program that once lost 80 consecutive games until they finally won when they ran into a pack of dimwits that sucked even more than they did. Hint: The game drew well over 5 fans who were treated to one of college football's greatest displays of punting.

9) The only player to ever lead the nation in rushing for U.N.L.V. later went on to play in a Super Bowl. Who is he? Hint: He was often seen making a fool of himself by dancing in the end zone after taking it in from the one inch line, after his teammates had just driven it 98 yards with this useless mulyak along for the joyride.

10) Name the three "schools" to have two winning streaks of 30 or more games in school history. Two are actually schools with real teachers and classes. The other is a crackhouse with a football field out back.

ANSWERS

COLLEGE FOOTBALL

6) Ed Marinaro in 1971 for Cornell, Marcus Allen in 1981 for USC, Barry Sanders in 1988 for Oklahoma State and Ladanian Thomlinson in 2000 for TCU.

7) Ed Marinaro of Cornell in 1970-71, Marshall Faulk of San Diego State 1991-92, Troy Davis of Iowa State 1995-96, Ricky Williams of Texas 1997-98 and Ladanian Thomlinson of TCU 1999-00.

8) Prairie View from 1989 to 1998.

9) Ickey Woods in 1987. He majored in slot machines with a minor in card shuffling and chip stacking.

10) Oklahoma with 47 and 31 game winning streaks, Penn 34 and 31 and Yale 37 and 31.

SCORE_____

DIVISION 1 COLLEGE FOOTBALL

11) Name the five tailbacks to lead the nation in rushing for USC. Hint: Four of them never murdered anyone................that we know of.

12) Name the only current NFL quarterback to lead the nation in passing two straight years while in college. The chances of him leading the NFL are about as good as seeing a nun hunched over center calling an audible as the Pope goes in motion in an attempt to shed the coverage of the Archbishop of Rome.

13) Only three quarterbacks in history have led the nation in passing and thrown for over 4,000 yards in their careers. Hint: All three were virgins playing for the same school. Name the school and the three blue-balls sufferers.

14) Which two glory hogs have scored over 30 TD's in a season? Hint: Several of the scores came on crucial fourth down plays in the waning seconds of 50 point blowouts when the opposing team had already hit the showers.

15) Which of the following stiffs never led the nation in passing? 1) Trent Dilfer 2) Danny Wuer(aw)ffel 3)Jim Har(Ain't no Sammy)baugh 4)Jeff Blake Hint: (This should narrow it down to four) He sucked as a pro.

ANSWERS

COLLEGE FOOTBALL

11) Marcus Allen in 1981, Charles White '79, O. J. Simp(leton)son '67-'68, Ricky Bell '75 and Mike Garrett '65.

12) Elvis Grbac for Michigan in 1991-'92. Grbac is German for garbage.

13) BYU—Jim McMahon in '80, Ty Detmer '89 and Steve Sarkisian '96.

14) Barry Sanders and Troy Edwards

15) Jeff Blake

SCORE_____

DIVISION 1 COLLEGE FOOTBALL

16) Name the QB who is the most efficient passer in NCAA history. Hints: He is one of the biggest wuss-bags to ever strap on a pair of cleats. His signature move is to look over the defensive formation with his mouth wide open, audible sixteen times, piss in his cup and then call time-out so he can beg the coach to remove him from the game.

17) Try to guess when the last time the winner of the Cotton Bowl became the national champion. Hint: The year was 1977, and the winning team was the usual cast of spoon fed dingbats who had everything handed to them the instant they left the womb.

18) Which three rushers managed to gain over 5,500 yards in their college careers without ever opening a textbook? (They were literate as several copies of Hustler and Screw magazine were found under their beds next to a hardened sock.)

19) Who set a NCAA season record with 54 TD passes, then went to the NFL and sucked a big bag of camel shit? Hints: His signature move was to drop back to get sacked, and then yell, "Holy Shit!!!!!!" as he spotted six wide open guys in the flat just as all the lights in his head went out. Late in his ephemeral career he would glare at opposing linemen while his heart pounded away inside his frail chest. Just before the ball was snapped he would glance down at his clipboard to make sure he had sent the right play in. He currently analyzes games on a tiny screen while sitting in the booth......on the New Jersey Turnpike.

ANSWERS

COLLEGE FOOTBALL

16) Danny Wuerffel of Florida.

17) Notre Dame in 1977 with lily white Joe Montana at quarterback.

18) Tony Dorsett, Ricky Williams and Ron Dayne

19) David Klingler of Houston University.

SCORE_____

DIVISION 1 COLLEGE FOOTBALL

20) Report to the nearest mental hospital if you know the name of the UCLA kicker who booted the most Field Goals in an NCAA season. Hint: He used to toe the ball, because his thigh muscle was all atrophied from lying around during practice with a tummy ache.

21) Name the annoying geek (NFL analyst) who shares the record for the longest pass play from scrimmage in a NCAA game. He did it for Rice University in 1977 and the play covered 99 yards. Hint: He is not a quarterback. He is a pain in the ass.

22) Name the last three Heisman Trophy winners to play for the eventual national champions. Hint: All three players have last names that begin with a letter in the alphabet. Extra hint: None of them are women.

23) Can you name the only Heisman Trophy winner in the 70's who played for the National Champions the year he won it? I can't.

24) Here's an easy one for all the numbskulls out there. Name the cold-blooded murderer who garnered the most points ever in Heisman Trophy voting. (Actually, the more I think about the slew of murders involving former and current NFL perps, this one is not really that easy).

ANSWERS

COLLEGE FOOTBALL

20) John Lee kicked 29 field goals in constant 85 degree balmy weather for UCLA in 1984. He tried out for the NFL but ran home when it started to snow. We tried to reach him for comment but his mother said he was coloring.

21) Chris Collinsworth

22) Charlie Ward for Florida State in 1993, Danny Wuerffel in '96 and Charles Woodson for Michigan in '97.

23) Tony Dorsett in 1976 for Pittsburgh. (I think).

24) O.J. Simp(leton)son (evidently voters felt threatened back in 1968 too).

SCORE_____

DIVISION 1 COLLEGE FOOTBALL

25) Name the player who, while playing strictly on defense, came the closest to winning the Heisman Trophy. Hint: He is now a defensive coordinator who wants to be head coach, but simply doesn't have a fat enough ass yet.

26) Name the two Heisman Trophy winning quarterbacks who later played for the New England Patriots, only to be discarded so they could flourish on a real football team. Hint: One has won two Super Bowls and the other has watched a bunch of Super Bowls, because his ability allows him to always be home for Christmas.

27) Who is the only two time winner of the Butkus Award? Hints: His NFL playing career was so lame he decided to go to Hollywood. He has plenty of acting (like a jackass) experience. The steroid abused pinhead also announced those things called "games" for the X"tinct"FL and chimed in with lurid commentary like "Wow, Whooeeeee, Unfuckingbelieveafuckingble!!"

28) Name the Penn State teammates who drank beers and ravaged the campus under the strict, watchful guise of Joe Paterno, then finished second and fourth in the Heisman voting one year in the 1990's.

29) One for the old coots—(if they're still hanging on) who won the first ever Heisman Trophy?

ANSWERS

COLLEGE FOOTBALL

25) Hugh Green. NFL insiders say Green needs a good four inches on his ass before he will even be considered. There are some skinny NFL coaches but you may have noticed that their skin color matches that of every owner in the league.

26) Doug "Home for the Holidays" Flutie and Jim Plunkett

27) Brian Bosworth for Oklahoma in 1985-86. Brian appeared in the movie "Stone Cold" which is a film about Brian's acting technique.

28) Ki jana Carter and Kerry Collins in 1994.

29) Jay Berwanger in 1935 for Chicago University. Berwanger used the trophy to pry rock hard kidney stones from his gall bladder.

SCORE_____

DIVISION 1 COLLEGE FOOTBALL

30) Iowa "Chicken Farm and Cow Milking School" (pronounced "University") quarterback Chuck Long lost the closest Heisman voting ever by a total of 45 points. He was beat by a man who actually possessed talent. Name the winner. Hint: The winner went on to have a great professional sports career. Note: Chuck Long was initially able to fool the Detroit Lions with some foolish rah-rah bullshit, but eventually the brilliant Lion brass looked at tapes and discovered he hadn't completed a pass in four years so they cut him.

ANSWERS

COLLEGE FOOTBALL

30) Bo Jackson of Auburn.

SCORE_____

OLYMPICS

1) Where was the first Olympic Games unfortunately held?

2) The record for the most gold medals in a Summer Olympics was set by what nation and in which Olympics? Hint: It is a city where you are likely to be pulled from your vehicle and beaten to a pulp by a transvestite crackhead.

3) The only city to host three Summer Olympics is also a dank sweat-hole where you are likely to get a beer bottle smashed over your head. Name this hooligan infested metropolis.

4) Because most humans refuse to take growth hormones and don't have a set of eight foot tall freaks for parents, only three nations have won a gold medal in Men's Basketball. Name these illustrious goon squads.

5) Who coached the last U.S. Men's Basketball team that failed to win a gold medal? Hint: He's also a horrendous announcer, unless you happen to enjoy monotone mumbling, run on sentences and inane commentary.

ANSWERS

OLYMPICS

1) Athens, Greece in 1896. One more reason to hate the Greeks.

2) The U.S. won 83 gold medals in the 1984 L.A. Olympics. The moral citizens of L.A. also garnered much gold by mugging, pick pocketing and looting.

3) London, England

4) Soviet Union, U.S.A and Yugoslavia

5) John Thompson in 1988. The mumbling bastard pronounces his name "Jahn Dumpsun."

SCORE_____

OLYMPICS

6) Name the only white player on the 1996 Dream Team II. Hints: He is the whitest player to ever play any professional sport. His signature move is to steal the ball because nobody can see him, then travel it up the court pushing his black opponent with one frail bony hand whilst palming and double dribbling it with the other. He makes repeated trips to the foul line because the refs get so sick of hearing him bitch and moan about the trials of the really bright white man.

7) Who is the only fighter to win three gold medals in Olympic heavyweight division boxing and then retire a destitute bum, because his country's leader chose to melt down the medals so he could purchase stogies and a lap dance?

8) Name the only U.S. heavyweight to win the gold medal by KO. Hints: A gap between his teeth (pronounced teef") allowed him to suck in more air than the average boxer. A gap between his ears allows him to receive large tax cuts.

9) Which hairless bodied "man" set the Olympic record for the 100 meter freestyle swimming event? Hint: He wisely chose the lane with the jet stream shooting out because it increases his velocity and he likes the way it feels on his scantily clad ass when he dives in.

10) The U.S. has dominated the 4 x 100 meter medley relay in swimming, having won it nine out of a possible ten times. The pharmacy was closed the year they didn't win. Name the only other country to put up with the horrendously long lines at CVS so they could shoot up and win this event.

ANSWERS

OLYMPICS

6) John Stockton

7) Teofilio Stevenson of Cuba

8) Ray Mercer in 1988.

9) Matt Biondi did it with the help of Nair, a buzz cut to his private area and a tiny outboard motor placed in his asshole.

10) Australia out-abused the competition in 1980.

SCORE_____

OLYMPICS

11) Who are the only two female lab rats to win two gold medals each in the 100 meter dash? Hint: For some reason each runner preferred to urinate from a standing position.

12) The most medals won in a single Olympics was eight by a Russian gymnast. Who is this pliable Communist bastard? Hint: His signature move was to lie on his back, curl himself into a ball and look seductively over the curvature of his ass at the judges while eating an overripe banana.

13) Which athlete sacrificed his liver, smooth skin and penis size to win the most gold medals in a single Summer Olympics?

14) Can you name the three U.S. "women" to win five medals in one Summer Olympics? Hint: Each woman trained so hard her breasts completely disappeared.

15) Who are the only two men to suffer through eight years of acne and road rage so they could win the Olympic decathlon twice? Hint: Each man trained by popping zits on his back to increase flexibility and then working on speed by car jacking people during intense bouts of road rage and then running away before the cops arrived.

ANSWERS

OLYMPICS

11) Wyomia Tyus in 1964 and 1968 and Gail Devers in 1992 and 1996.

12) Aleksandr Dityatin with 3 gold, 4 silver and 1 bronze in 1980.

13) Mark Spitz won 7 in 1976.

14) Shirley Babashoff in swimming in 1976, Mary Lou Retton '84 and Shannon Miller '92 both did it in gymnastics.

15) Daley Thompson from Great Britain and Bob Mathias of the U.S.

SCORE_____

OLYMPICS

16) The record for most gold medals by one country in a Winter Olympics is thirteen. (The record for the fewest is none and is held by every nation in Africa.) Name the country and the host nation where it took place.

17) Because real men are off drinking in the winter, three fellas have gone out and won three gold medals each for alpine skiing. Who did this while the entire world barely batted an eyelash?

18) Bjorn Dahlie has won the most individual gold medals in Winter Olympic history. He is now attempting something even more difficult, finding someone who gives a shit. What event did he dull our senses with in his career?

19) Name the frozen-titted American woman who has won the most medals for the U.S. in Winter Olympic competition. Hint: She is considered an Winter Olympic hero, which means that when she walks down the street with her medals clanking around her neck people point at her and go "who the hell is that noisy bimbo?"

20) The answer to question 19 also shares the honor of most Winter Olympic gold medals won for the U.S. with what leotard-clad wussbag? Hint: This thunder thighed speed skater blew away the competition with a combination of strength and speed. The strength was the result of hours in the weight room. The speed was likely purchased from a dealer on the corner of 4th and Madison.

ANSWERS

OLYMPICS

16) USSR at the Innsbruck Olympics in 1976.

17) Jean Claude Killy, Toni Sailer and Alberto Tomba

18) Fear of Heights Skiing (Cross Country)

19) Bonnie Blair with 6 (Five gold and one meaningless (bronze))

20) Eric Heiden (5 gold)

SCORE_____

OLYMPICS

---

21) Can you name the country that hosted the first Winter Olympics in 1924? Hint: The inhabitants are renowned assholes today, back then and forevermore.

22) Only three U.S. men have barreled down the side of a mountain with their eyes closed and shit pouring out of their asses, then opened them to find they had won gold medals in an Olympic skiing event. Who are these odorous heroes of the slopes?

23) Only once has the U.S. won the most overall medals in a Winter Olympics. What year was this and where did it take place? Hint: The U.S. was the host, so the conspirators (judges) were able to turn in their scorecards two weeks before the ceremonial torch was lit.

24) On two other occasions a nation won the most medals in a Winter Olympics that it fixed (pronounced "hosted"). Which nation accomplished this, most likely by switching it's athletes' urine samples with those of the local priests and nuns?

25) Which of the following countries has ignored basic human rights and more importantly, never won a gold medal in men's or women's skiing? Russia, Germany, Sweden, or Canada

ANSWERS

OLYMPICS

21) France in 1924

22) Phil Mahre in 1984, Bill Johnson in '84 and Tommy Moe in '94.

23) Lake Placid in 1932 with a total of 12. (Six gold and six other useless elements off the periodic chart).

24) Norway did it in Lillehammer—1994 and Oslo—1952.

25) Russia

SCORE_____

OLYMPICS

26) Which country has never won a gold medal in bobsledding because its' athletes have a fear of speed, death and wet frozen undies? Hint: The sled is often seen careening down the hill carrying terrified men barfing off the side of the craft. Is it France, Great Britain, Switzerland, or the U.S.?

27) Name the five U.S. "men" to throw their dignity out the window by donning pink flower-emblazoned body suits in order to win endorsement deals from Proctor and Gamble (pronounced "Olympic gold in figure skating"). Hint: Several later regained their dignity by doing splits in a tutu and then getting spun around like a top by some hairy-chested clown in a tin foil suit.

28) Name the five U.S. women to win Olympic gold in figure skating by exposing their panty lines to a group of salivating judges.

29) How many gold medals has the United States won in toothless figure skating (ice hockey)?

ANSWERS

OLYMPICS

26) France

27) Dick Button, Hayes Alan Jenkins, David Jenkins, Scott Hamilton and Brian Boitano.

28) Carol Heiss (Garter), Tenly Albright (Depends), Dorothy Hamill (Bikini bottom), Kristi Yamaguchi (Fishnet) and Tara Lipinski (underoos).

29) The men won in 1960 and 1980 and the women (don't forget them you chauvinist pig) in 1998.

SCORE_____

OLYMPICS

30) Three showoffs have won medals in both Winter and Summer Olympics because they enjoyed rare hobbies, had huge amounts of time on their hands and thought it would be a bigger deal than it actually was. Match the selfish headline grabber with the hobbies they competed in and name the only one to win gold in both pastimes.

1. Eddie Eagan

2. Jacob Tullin Thams

3. Christa Luding Rothenburger

A. Boxing—Bobsled

B. Speed Skating—Sprint Cycling

C. Ski Jumping – Yachting

ANSWERS

OLYMPICS

30) 1-A , 2-C, 3-B. Eddie Eagan won 2 gold medals, but to this day nobody is impressed because a corpse could win a medal in bobsledding. All you have to do is put a plastic runner on the bottom of the casket, and have a bunch of pallbearers shove the damn thing down the hill.

SCORE_____

WUSSY SPORTS
(SOCCER, GOLF, TENNIS)

1) While nations like the U.S. are out kicking ass in world wars, five shitbag countries have placed their backward assed priorities on winning more than one World Cup in soccer. Name these whacked out sections of the planet.

2) Do you know the last South American soccer team to win the World Cup on European soil, then make it back to the team plane just ahead of an angry mob of knife wielding hooligans?

3) Which player has scored a record 14 goals in his World Cup career? Hints: A total of 16 have been scored in World Cup history. His signature move after scoring a goal was to run over to the stands and shake his booty at a crowd of fans who were sound asleep at the time. He would then run over to his coach and hug him so tight the coach would wake up shouting "Ooooh Martha, I knew you'd come back to me you greasy thing you!"

4) In the 1958 World Cup final, a record number of goals were scored by the winning team, creating such excitement several fans had to be taken to nearby hospitals and placed on defibrillators. How many did the winners score? Hint: It is far from being a double digit number.

5) Which college has won the most NCAA Men's Soccer titles, despite the fact that nobody gives a shit? Hint: The term "men" is used loosely as soccer players tend to prance about in silk shorts that show off their shaved navels, ultra smooth legs and tight little asses.

ANSWERS

WUSSY SPORTS

1) Brazil has won four titles, Italy and West Germany have each won three and Argentina and Uruguay have each won two. All five nations have their armies on red alert in the event of a bad call or a trip in the penalty box.

2) Brazil won in Sweden in 1958.

3) Gerd Muller of West Germany did it by averaging just under a goal per year during his fifteen year career.

4) Brazil caused the scoreboard to short circuit by scoring five goals. The five goals continue to baffle scientists and fans to this very day. Additional footnote: The opposing goalie was immediately flown home and executed by firing squad.

5) St. Louis University has won 10 while an entire nation snoozes.

SCORE_____

WUSSY SPORTS

6) Who are the only four tycoons to win the U.S. Open and the British Open in the same year without breaking a sweat? Hint: Each man celebrated by tossing back several sips of chardonnay and then staying up all night reading poems and soliloquies.

7) Only two "men" have ever won back to back Masters titles. One of them is an old fart. The other is on his way to coot-dom. Both looked horrible in green. Who are these two gutless scoundrels?

8) Who is the last man to drink, curse and smoke his way to winning back to back U.S. Opens? Hint: His signature move is to take the pen from an autograph seeker and chuck it as far as a non-athlete can throw. He then grabs the pad of paper and heads for the men's room so he can wipe the caviar from his ass.

9) The two lowest rounds in U.S. Open history were both scored at Baltusrol C. C. in Springfield, New Jersey (formerly a pitch and putt). Which two golfers achieved this low round?

10) Can you name the three golf addicts to win ten or more majors in their careers, while their families were placed on the shelf and left to rot with all the old trophies?

ANSWERS

WUSSY SPORTS

6) Ben Hogan (1953), Lee Trevino (1971), Tom Watson (1982) and Tiger Woods (2000).

7) Jack Nicklaus (the old fart) in 1965-66 and Nick Faldo in 1989-90.

8) Curtis Strange in 1988-89.

9) Jack Nicklaus and Lee Janzen with a 272 score. Each man used only a wedge and a putter the entire round.

10) Jack Nicklaus (20), Bobby Jones (13) and Walter Hagen (11).

SCORE_____

WUSSY SPORTS

11) Who are the only two golfers to win three of the four majors (Masters, U.S. Open, British, PGA) in one year? Hint: One did it with talent, the other did it by intimidating his opponent and consistently farting on his back swing.

12) Because men aren't allowed in the ladies shower we have to assume that four "women" have won over 10 majors in their career. Who or what accomplished this? Each gal has long muscular sexy legs that extend up to a region that has had biologists baffled for years.

13) A total of six wool-clad bungholes have each cashed over 50 PGA Tournament winner's checks, then flipped homeless people the bird on their way out of the bank. Name these circle account members. Hint: Each of the pompous douche bags has put the money to good use by lighting large areas of land on fire and killing a bunch of furry animals (pronounced "building a golf course") so a bunch of old farts can wander around looking for some stupid white balls.

14) Two members of the 1999 U.S. Ryder Cup Squad hold NCAA marks for most Division 1 individual championships with three. Who are these two cowards? Hint: You may recall them making utter nitwits of themselves on the green in Brookline, Massachusetts.

15) Who was the last limp-wristed men's tennis player to win three Grand Slam Tournaments in one year? Hints: His typical game plan was to lull his opponent to sleep by slapping 20 m.p.h. serves over the net, while simultaneously babbling on and on about how his children were doing in school. He also had his wife walk behind his opponent wearing nothing but a racket cover.

ANSWERS

WUSSY SPORTS

11) Ben Hogan in 1953 and Tiger Woods in 2000.

12) Louise Suggs (16), Patty Berg (13), Mickey Wright (13) and Babe Didrickson Zahairyass (12).

13) Byron Nelson, Sam Snead, Jack Nicklaus (I'm sick of seeing his name too), Billy Casper, Arnold Palmer and Ben Hogan

14) Phil Mickelson and Ben Crenshaw.

15) Mats Wilander in 1988

SCORE_____

WUSSY SPORTS

16) Which tournament did the player in question 15 not win because his wife was busy that weekend dancing on tables and straddling the laps of boorish drunks?

17) There is only one tournament that Pete Sampras(s) has not won amongst the four Grand Slam events. Which one causes him to play like a wino?

18) Which major has Pete Sampras(shole) balled his eyes out after (won) the most times? Pete cries because he knows that if there were any good players around today, he would be wearing a paper hat and taking my drive-thru order at McDonalds.

19) Name the two women who have pranced around with their skirt up over their head en route to 20 Grand Slam singles tennis titles. Hint: One wore pink panties with white lace, the other wore white men's briefs with stains.

20) Name the men's tennis player who has paddled his way to the most singles matches all time with 109. Hint: The bodies of four line judges were recently discovered in his basement.

21) Name the three jaw-jutted androids (pronounced "female tennis players") who have won over 100 singles tennis tournaments. Hint: One is easy, the other two are a little tougher to get in bed.

ANSWERS

WUSSY SPORTS

16) Wimbledon

17) French Open

18) He has flooded the streets of Wimbledon with his crocodile tears a total of six times.

19) Margaret Smith Court (24) and Steffi Graf (22)

20) Jimmy Connors (the line judges weren't identifiable).

21) Martina Navritilova with 167, Chris Evert with 154 and Steffi Graf with 105.

SCORE_____

WUSSY SPORTS

22) Because the average line judge is a cockeyed douche bag, only two men have been able to overcome atrocious calls to win three consecutive U.S. Open tennis titles. Who are they?

23) Who is the last auto racer to avoid a fiery death and win back to back Daytona 500's? Hint: His racing strategy was to strap himself in the vehicle, set the cruise on 165 and then spend the next three hours defecating himself in a complete state of fear as the car whizzed around the track.

24) Even though the car does all the work, one man took credit for winning two Daytona 500's from the pole position. Who? Hint: He sat in the front seat listening to the radio (won) in 1985 and 1987.

25) Name the two father-son combinations to win Rookie of the Year in the Indy circuit. Hint: Both sons were conceived in the back seat of the father's car during a pit stop. The crew pitched in by polishing the father's ball joints, pumping his ass up and down and oiling the mother's G spot.

26) Of the three Triple Crown races in horse racing, which one is the most boring (longest)? Hint: The crowd is often awoken from a deep slumber by a shrieking horse being fired upon by three assholes with shotguns. After a moment of silence for the deceased thoroughbred (if you consider 10,000 drunks screaming "get that filthy animal off the fucking track" as quiet) the grieving owner tries to overcome his tremendous loss (of money) by going down to the track to see if anyone's interested in purchasing a vial of horse sperm.

ANSWERS

WUSSY SPORTS

22) John McEnroe from 1979-81 and Ivan Lendl from 1985-87.

23) Sterling Martin

24) Bill Elliot

25) Mario and Michael Andretti (1965 and 1984 respectively) and Bill and Billy Vukovich III (1968 and 1988).

26) The Belmont Stakes (1.5 miles)

SCORE_____

WUSSY SPORTS

---

27) Name the only horse to win the Triple Crown, then plunge its' member into another horse to produce screams of pleasure and yet another Triple Crown winner with a really good chance of being shot later in life.

28) The last Triple Crown winner (Affirmed) came in just ahead of the same horse in all three races. Because horses don't have opposable thumbs the runner up wasn't able to shoot himself in the skull. Because horses don't wear condoms the loser went on to sire several more horses. Name the losing horse.

29) Who is the only jockey to put his pint sized, hemorrhoid-ridden bony ass on two Triple Crown winning horses? Hint: The silk clad nitwit needed 4 telephone books stacked under his butt so he could see over the horses head. He also never got laid...........for free.

30) In which stadium did Brandi Chastain garner millions in endorsements by exposing her A cup breasts, flat ass and manly arms after the U.S. Women's soccer team defeated China to win the World Cup? Hint: It is one of the largest eyesores (pronounced "stadiums") in the U.S. Several fans in the cheap seats glared at Brandi's chest and muttered "if that asshole takes his pants off I'm outta here."

ANSWERS

WUSSY SPORTS

27) Gallant Fox nailed Flambino to produce Omaha and a very messy stable.

28) Alydar

29) Eddie Arcaro in 1941 aboard Whirlaway and in 1948 aboard Citation. Neither horse had any idea he was sitting atop them.

30) The Rose Bowl

SCORE_____

MISCELLANEOUS

---

1) Only three NHL franchises have made 20 or more Stanley Cup Finals appearances. Name them. Hint: Two are in Canada where real hockey is played and championships are celebrated with parades. The other is in the U.S. where they play a brand of roller derby and championships are celebrated by setting people on fire and raping any broad you can get your mitts on.

2) True or false. In the 1986 AFC playoffs horse-toothed hillbilly John Elway drove the Broncos 98 yards in the closing minutes for the winning touchdown vs. Cleveland.

3) Name the first wild card* team to win a Super Bowl. (*sucky) Hint: It was another tremendous commercial filled ballgame whose outcome wasn't decided until very late in the flight of the opening kickoff. Later, when asked who won the game, most fans replied "Bud Light."

4) Millions of overweight dumb-assed Americans have foolishly watched three other NFL teams go to the Super Bowl as TV sponsored wild card entries. Who are these teams?

5) There have been only two NFL champions to win 18 games (including playoffs) in a season. Which two teams did it? Hint: Both teams utilized the salary cap and their mob connections to threaten the lives of (pronounced "lure") players to their organizations.

ANSWERS

MISCELLANEOUS

1) Toronto, Detroit and Montreal

2) False. He drove them 98 yards for the tying score. Denver won in OT.

3) Oakland in 1980.

4) New England (1985), Oakland (1980) and Tennessee (1999)

5) Chicago (1985) and San Francisco (1984 and 1989)

SCORE_____

MISCELLANEOUS

6) Of all the teams to lose the Super Bowl, which one had the highest winning percentage (including playoffs) in that season? Hint: Several gamblers had their legs snapped the next morning. I managed to get away and have been on the run ever since.

7) Only two men have fought both Muhammad Ali and Mike Tyson without getting anally violated. Who are these butt-corked fighters? Hint: Each man prepared for the Tyson bout by donning a chastity belt and then sparring in a hot tub against a sex crazed inmate with a lisp.

8) Who holds the record for the most RBI's in a decade with 1,403? Hints: A decade is a span of ten years (ie. 1920's, 1930's etc.). Also, instead of steroids, he built up his arms the old fashioned way—by beating people up and then hoisting their wives on his back and carrying their writhing bodies up to his trashed hotel room.

9) Only four coaches in NFL history have guided two different teams to the Super Bowl, because most of the other coaches have no idea what the hell they're doing. Who are these four mediocre legends?

10) What pro football stadium has the largest seating capacity? Hint: Due to a lot of past problems with drunks, the stadium stops serving beer when the kegs run dry. Customers are also limited to purchasing two 80 oz. flagons per visit to the beer stand. The stands are located at the end of every row. Vodka shots are available at the courtesy gate. Anyone smoking marijuana will get really baked. There are also two auxiliary cops on duty in case things really get out of hand.

ANSWERS

MISCELLANEOUS

6) Baltimore in 1969.

7) Larry Holmes and Trevor Berbick

8) Jimmie Foxx with 1,403 in the 1930's.

9) Dan Reeves (ATL and DEN), Bill Parcells (NE and NYG), Don Shula (MIA and BALT) and Dick Vermeil (PHI and ST. LOUIS).

10) Pontiac Silverdome. 80,335 drunks are able to squeeze in the facility to watch the Barry Sanders-less Lions drag their lazy asses up and down the field in a pathetic attempt to impersonate a football team.

SCORE_____

MISCELLANEOUS

11) A total of three Division 1 football stadiums have seating capacities to house over 100,000 obnoxious assholes. Which three are primed for a monumental human catastrophe, hopefully occurring in the next few years?

12) Which of the following trophies has the highest monetary value (based on appraisal figures)? Stanley Cup, Americas Cup, Commissioner's Trophy (baseball), Ryder Cup, or Midget Tossing Champions Cup

13) An Olympic gold medal is comprised of what two elements? Hint: The elements are not liquids or gases.

14) When a boxer loses a title fight, does he by rule have to forfeit his belt to the winner or can he keep it to impress whoever happens to be his wife that particular week?

15) Which of the following weighs the most? Lombardi Trophy, The World Cup, Davis Cup, Heisman Trophy, or a bucket of William "The Refrigerator" Perry's shit

16) Does the Heisman Trophy winner get to keep the trophy for life?

ANSWERS

MISCELLANEOUS

11) Michigan Stadium, Ohio Stadium & Neyland Stadium (Tennessee).

12) America's Cup ($250,000)

13) It is made of silver and gilded with gold.

14) No. A new belt is made for the winner.

15) Davis Cup weighs over 400 pounds. FYI: Perry's shit—345 lbs

16) Yes, although it can be auctioned off after a civil lawsuit finds you guilty of murder.

SCORE_____

MISCELLANEOUS

17) The Vince Lombardi Trophy features a football on top of a stand. Is the football smaller than regulation size, larger than regulation or the same? Hint: The Lombardi trophy is the one that the Ruler of all Mankind (NFL Commissioner) hands to the coach of the Super Bowl champs as he whispers "F you" under his breath. Each egotistical jackass forces a bogus smile for the cameras, then both disappear behind closed doors and begin beating the shit out of one another because the league made billions, but money can't buy you love.

18) Time Magazine's Man of the Year has twice gone to pompous asses with sports credentials and or affiliations. Who are the two men? Hints: One is an imperious scoundrel who plays an asshole on TV. The other seems cool, but I've made that mistake before.

19) Name the two hockey players who have had their numbers retired by two teams. Hint: They were good players. Both had sons who, despite a dearth of talent, were able to make NHL teams because of a thing called nepotism. (Reference: See White House; George Bush. Also actors; Baldwin and Fonda).

20) The Boston Celtics have retired the most numbers (20) in NBA history. Portland, despite having a history that is about as legendary as the sixth grade team at Buttcrack Elementary, is next with eight because you gotta hang something from the rafters. How many Trailblazers can you name?

ANSWERS

MISCELLANEOUS

17) Regulation

18) Ted Turner and Peter Ueberroth

19) #9 of Gordie Howe (Detroit and Hartford) and Bobby Hull (Winnipeg and Chicago).

20) Larry Weinberg?? (your guess is as good as mine) #1, Dave Twardzik #13, Larry Steele #15, Maurice Lucas(s) #20, Bill Walton #32, Lloyd Neal #36, Geoff Petrie #45, and Jack Ramsey #77. How sad!!

SCORE_____

MISCELLANEOUS

21) Who is the only baseball player to have his number retired by three teams, because he constantly wore out his welcome with his arrogance and foul locker room gas? Hint: His signature pitch was a 99 m.p.h. heater that would start in on the batter's penis and then break upward towards other life threatening areas of the body. He could also change speeds by throwing a 112 m.p.h. steamer that would start at the batter's head and stay right on course, shattering bones and flesh in it's wake. He was able to stay in the game after hitting people by correctly pointing out to the umpire that he sucked as a pitcher.

22) Which offensive skill position is represented the most in the NFL Hall of Fame? Hint: Center is not a skill position as it takes no skill to shove a needle into your buttock and then bend over the football while the quarterback sticks his chapped frozen hands up your sore anus.

23) Try to name the only placekicker in the NFL Hall of Fame. Hint: He's as bald as a walnut and most likely a queer. His signature move on a kickoff was to pretend his foot was frozen to the ground so he wouldn't have to go down and make a tackle. His cowardice and gender were uncovered when he was found douching himself with potpourri in the locker room before a playoff game.

24) Among NFL coaches with 105 or more victories, only four have a winning percentage of over 70% in the regular season. A few cowardly got out of the game just as their team headed down the road to suckdom. Two were warned by their bosses to never venture onto the field alone with a clipboard in their hands. Who are these yellowbellied gurus of the gridiron?

ANSWERS

MISCELLANEOUS

21) Nolan Ryan (Houston and Texas #34 and California #30)

22) Running Back

23) Jan Stenurud

24) George Allen, George Seifert, Vince Lombardi and John Madden

SCORE_____

MISCELLANEOUS

---

25) Who am I? I coached a team to a Super Bowl win and also won two NFL titles and one AFL title before the merger. Despite these impressive credentials my overall career record is only 134-130. My favorite foods are steak, hot dogs, beer and sausage. Surprise, surprise—my heart exploded.

26) Match the ballplayer with the year he won the MVP and the size of his ego.

Jeff Burroughs	1971	Black hole-like
Vida Blue	1977	Humongous
Rod Carew	1974	Tiny
Reggie Jackson	1973	Gargantuan

27) Who is the only football coach to lose three AFC Title games in a row and a total of six in his career? Hint: He is a fat shit who is afraid to fly. Obvious question: Who wouldn't be afraid to board a plane when weighing well over three bills?

28) Which jockey rode Affirmed to the Triple Crown— Eddie Arcaro, John Lively, Steve Cauthen, Jean Cruguet, Tattoo, Beetlejuice or Dumpy from the Seven Dwarfs?

ANSWERS

MISCELLANEOUS

25) Weeb Ewbank

26) Burroughs—1974—humongous, Blue—'71—gargantuan, Carew- '77-
tiny and Jackson—'73—black hole-like.

27) John Madden for the Raiders in 1969, '70, '73, '74, '75 and '77.

28) Steve Cauthen came across the finish line on Affirmed breathing nor-
mally and then hogged all the credit after the horse nearly killed itself
(raced to victory).

SCORE_____

MISCELLANEOUS

29) Can you recall what place Nancy "Why me" Kerrigan and Tonya "Hubcap" Harding finished in Figure Skating at the Lillehammer Olympics in 1994?

30) Who won the famous chess match between IBM's Deep Blue Computer and Gary Kasparov? (This is the lamest possible way I could end the book.)

ANSWERS

MISCELLANEOUS

29) Kerrigan came in second and Harding came in eighth. In life both came in nine million two hundred eighty five thousandth.

30) Kasparov bored the computer to death (won) 4 games to 2

SCORE_____

THANK GOD (THE END)

ABOUT THE AUTHOR

Paul Nardizzi is a stand-up comedian who performs around the country and recently won the 2001 Boston Comedy Competition. He has made numerous appearances on NBC's Late Night with Conan O'Brien and is the author of *602 Reasons to be PISSED OFF......Volume 1* which has sold well over three copies. Paul lives in Framingham, Massachusetts with his wife and four children. He hopes this book made you laugh.

Breinigsville, PA USA
06 December 2009
228741BV00001B/74/A